MW01492190

The Roac
and .

In the school of discipleship, you never graduate. You are forever growing as a follower of Christ. For a Christian, the key is to continue to grow, and to be committed to growth. When you stop growing, you start dying.

Imagine your Christian growth as a journey along a mountain trail. Sometimes the trail winds along beautiful valleys. At other times, you are trying to climb a difficult ledge. Your location on the trail is not as important as whether or not you are moving forward.

This guide has been designed to help you and your Mentor see where you are on your journey and to help you see how to move forward into maturity and ministry. Think of it as a tool that helps you determine your location on a map. With that in mind, take some time to complete this guide as honestly as possible so that you know exactly where you are and where you need to go.

If you have been a member of a cell group for a while, you are probably looking ahead for the next steps that God has for you. This *Journey Guide* will help you take those steps. If this is your first exposure to life in a cell group but you have been a part of the church for a some time, you need to know how you can fully contribute to the group. This tool will point you in the direction of becoming an effective minister both inside and outside the group.

After you have completed this guide, your Mentor will arrange a personal time of sharing with you. You will be able to share insights you've gained, and your Mentor will be able to help you plot your next step. It is always good to have a partner in your spiritual journey.

The questions in this booklet are designed to help you evaluate your progress in the journey. Some of the questions are multiple choice. On these, feel free to check each statement that is true for you. Other questions are open ended and ask you to write out your response. None of the questions have right or wrong answers. This is your *Journey Guide* and the only "right" answers are those that reflect your heart and your journey.

At the end of the *Guide*, you will find a Journey Map to help you plot the next steps of your route. Be open to the Holy Spirit as He shows you areas in your life that still need work. He is always by your side, ready to help you when you call on Him. Your Mentor is committed to your success, so you can trust him. He or she will stand by you and aid you as you continue your adventure with God.

Now go for it!

Your Walk with Christ

BRIEFLY DESCRIBE HOW YOU INITIALLY CAME TO KNOW CHRIST AS YOUR LORD
AND SAVIOR.

_____

_____

_____

_____

_____

I CAN DESCRIBE MY CHRISTIAN LIFE THUS FAR AS:
Check [✓] each statement that is true for you:
- ☐ Exciting — I am very thankful.
- ☐ Powerful — I have felt God make Himself real to me.
- ☐ Dramatic — I have experienced many changes in my life.
- ☐ Difficult — I have been struggling.
- ☐ Other: _____

DESCRIBE YOUR ANSWER IN A FEW WORDS:

_____

_____

_____

_____

_____

HOW OFTEN DO YOU SPEND TIME WITH GOD?
- ☐ Daily — I spend time alone with God every day.
- ☐ Consistently — I spend time with God about 5 times a week.
- ☐ Occasionally — I spend time with God when I remember.
- ☐ Rarely — I can't seem to find the time.

THINK OF A RECENT PERSONAL TIME WITH GOD THAT WAS SIGNIFICANT. BRIEFLY
DESCRIBE WHAT HAPPENED IN YOUR TIME WITH THE LORD.

_____

_____

_____

_____

_____

RECENTLY, WHEN YOU SPEND TIME READING THE WORD, HOW DO YOU FEEL?

☐ Empowered — It feeds my spirit, and I feel closer to God.
☐ Enlightened — It gives me insight into areas of my life I need to improve.
☐ Troubled — I am not sure how to apply the Bible to my life.
☐ Frustrated — I have difficulty understanding the Bible.
☐ Bored — It does not keep my attention.
☐ Other: _____

RATE HOW HELPFUL THE FOLLOWING ARE IN GETTING THE WORD OF GOD INTO YOUR LIFE:

Give it a [4] if it is extremely helpful, a [3] if it is moderately helpful, [2] if it is slightly helpful, and a [1] if it is not at all helpful.

_____ Listening to the Sunday sermon.
_____ Discussing the sermon with others.
_____ Spending time with your Mentor.
_____ Attending training classes.
_____ Reading devotional books or listening to instructional recordings.
_____ Studying the Bible.
_____ Memorizing the Word of God.

HOW DO YOU TYPICALLY RESPOND TO NEGATIVE CIRCUMSTANCES THAT ARE OUT OF YOUR CONTROL?

☐ I worry.
☐ I get angry.
☐ I ignore the circumstances and act like nothing is wrong.
☐ I get to work and try to fix it.
☐ I increase my time in prayer.
☐ Other: _____

HOW DO YOU RESPOND WHEN YOU FIND YOURSELF WITH PEOPLE WHO ARE ACTING IN COMPROMISING WAYS (I.E. LYING, GOSSIPING, DRUNKEN, ETC.), ?

☐ I go along, but I don't participate.
☐ I feel drawn into the activity and then I feel guilty.
☐ I walk away.
☐ I tell them that what they are doing is wrong.
☐ I cut off the relationship with those people.
☐ Other: _____

Your Relationships

Check [✓] each statement that is true for you:

HOW DO YOU DESCRIBE YOUR FAMILY?

☐ Close — we enjoy being together and sharing with each other.
☐ Harmonious — we get along but don't have deep relationships.
☐ Uncommunicative — no one shares about their lives with others.
☐ Distrustful — the relationships in my family are mainly grudges and bitterness.
☐ Other: _____

BRIEFLY DESCRIBE YOUR ANSWER:

_____
_____
_____
_____
_____

WHICH OF THESE BEST DESCRIBES YOU WHEN YOU ARE WITH CLOSE FRIENDS OR FAMILY?

☐ Natural — I am able to relax and be myself.
☐ Open — I feel free to talk about what I think and believe.
☐ Passive — I am the quiet one who waits for others to share.
☐ Struggling — I don't always stand up for what I believe.
☐ Discontented — I feel like no one understands me.
☐ Other: _____

WHICH OF THESE BEST DESCRIBES YOUR RELATIONSHIPS WITH OTHERS?

☐ I am sensitive to the feelings of others; people see me as an understanding person.
☐ I am unable to share deeply; my relationships with others are generally superficial.
☐ I react badly to others; I get upset easily and have trouble resolving conflicts.
☐ I have no problem resolving conflicts with other people when they arise.
☐ I want to fit in, so I have trouble sharing my Christian convictions when I am with my non-Christian friends.

Testing Your Bible Knowledge (1)

> *Instructions:* Write the numbers of items in Column 2 which properly relate to items in Column 1.

____	Gideon	1.	A pool of water.
11	Lot	2.	Holy Spirit given.
16	Paul	3.	Sons of Noah.
10	James	4.	Discipled Elisha.
____	John	5.	A judge of Israel.
14	Aaron	6.	Cut off a man's ear.
____	Capernaum	7.	Like a thief in the night.
15	Lazarus	8.	Father of lies.
3	Shem, Ham, Japheth	9.	Sword of the Spirit.
1	Bethesda	10.	Half brother of Jesus.
6	Peter	11.	Abraham's nephew.
4	Elijah	12.	Jesus lived there.
____	Second coming of Jesus	13.	Patmos prisoner.
____	Pentecost	14.	Brother of Moses.
8	Satan	15.	Raised from the dead.
____	Word of God	16.	Discipled Timothy.

Check your answers — See bottom of page 10.

Testing Your Bible Knowledge (2)

Instructions: Write the numbers of items in Column 2 which properly relate to items in Column 1.

____ Joseph

____ Deborah

____ Bethany

____ Bartholomew

____ Abigail

____ Bethel

____ Demas

____ Nehemiah

____ David

____ Job

____ Holy of Holies

____ Barnabas

____ Meshach

____ Satan

____ Darius

____ Tarsus

1. A disciple who forsook Paul.

2. The man who did not forsake God in the time of distress and trouble.

3. A man after God's own heart.

4. Threw Daniel into the den of lions.

5. Place where Paul the Apostle was born.

6. An "encourager" in the early church.

7. The man who led the rebuilding of the wall around Jerusalem.

8. The accuser of our brothers.

9. The dwelling place of the Ark of the Covenant.

10. Village where Mary and Martha lived.

11. Thrown into the fiery furnace.

12. A judge of Israel.

13. The Israelite who became Pharaoh's assistant.

14. Where Jacob had a vision of angels on a ladder.

15. David's wife.

16. A disciple of Jesus.

Check your answers — See bottom of page 10.

Your Ministry

Check [✓] each statement that is true for you:

WHAT PREVIOUS MINISTRY TRAINING HAVE YOU COMPLETED?
- ☐ A new believer's course.
- ☐ A basic discipleship course.
- ☐ A course on spiritual gifts.
- ☐ An evangelism course.
- ☐ A leadership training course.
- ☐ Other: _____

WHAT MINISTRY ACTIVITIES HAVE YOU PARTICIPATED IN?

_____   _____
_____   _____
_____   _____
_____   _____
_____   _____

DESCRIBE YOUR CHURCH ATTENDANCE:

☐ Sunday celebration	☐ Regular	☐ Irregular
☐ Training classes	☐ Regular	☐ Irregular
☐ Cell meeting	☐ Regular	☐ Irregular
☐ Other cell activities	☐ Regular	☐ Irregular
☐ Other: _____	☐ Regular	☐ Irregular

IN THE PAST YEAR, HOW HAS GOD USED YOU TO TOUCH THE LIVES OF THOSE WHO DON'T KNOW JESUS YET?
- ☐ I led several people to the Lord.
- ☐ I led at least one person to the Lord.
- ☐ I share my testimony but no one has responded to it yet.
- ☐ I brought people to church or cell group activities.
- ☐ I found it hard to bring people to church or group activities.
- ☐ All my friends who are interested in Jesus have already made commitments — I do not have any more non-believing friends.
- ☐ I don't feel confident to share with others about Jesus.
- ☐ Other: _____

7

THINK OF A TIME WHEN GOD USED YOU TO MINISTER TO OR CARE FOR SOMEONE ELSE. DESCRIBE WHAT HAPPENED.

_____
_____
_____
_____

BRIEFLY DESCRIBE A SITUATION WHEN YOU USED YOUR FINANCIAL RESOURCES TO BENEFIT SOMEONE ELSE. HOW DID YOU FEEL ABOUT DOING THIS?

_____
_____
_____
_____
_____
_____

THINK OF THE LAST TIME YOU SHARED YOUR FAITH WITH A NON-CHRISTIAN. BRIEFLY DESCRIBE HOW YOU FELT AND WHAT HAPPENED.

_____
_____
_____
_____

IN WHAT KIND OF MINISTRY ACTIVITIES DO YOU DESIRE TO PARTICIPATE?

_____   _____
_____   _____
_____   _____
_____   _____

WHAT ARE SOME THINGS YOU LIKE TO DO TO SERVE OTHERS?
☐ Organize activities where people can get together.
☐ Cook a meal for a group of people.
☐ Perform behind the scenes tasks that no one sees.
☐ Talk with people about their struggles and problems.
☐ Reach out to people who feel like they don't belong.
☐ Pray for people even though they don't know I do it.
☐ Other: _____
☐ Other: _____

Lingering Struggles

"Before we received Christ, we were slaves to sin. But because of Christ's work on the cross, sin's power over us has been broken. Satan has no right of ownership or authority over us. He is a defeated foe, but he is committed to keeping us from realizing that. He knows he can block your effectiveness as a Christian if he can deceive you in believing that you are nothing but a product of your past, subject to sin, prone to failure, and controlled by your habits. As long as he can confuse you and blind you with his dark lies, you won't be able to see that the chains which once bound you are broken.

"You are free in Christ, but if the devil can deceive you into believing you are not, you won't experience the freedom which is your inheritance." — Neil Anderson

This is the good news — you can be set free! There is victory in Christ. Check [✓] the following areas where you still struggle. This will help you identify the places in your life where you need God to lead you into freedom.

THE FOLLOWING INNER EMOTIONS STILL BOTHER ME:

- ☐ Guilt — I feel guilty even when I'm not wrong.
- ☒ Anger — I get angry easily and sometimes violently.
- ☒ Anxiety — I worry over circumstances outside of my control.
- ☒ Depression — I feel inadequate and worthless.
- ☐ Bitterness — I find it hard to forgive and forget.
- ☐ Other: _____

MY THOUGHTS ARE FILLED WITH THE FOLLOWING:

- ☐ Lustful images.
- ☒ Negative self-image.
- ☒ Worry about the future.
- ☐ Blasphemous thoughts toward God.
- ☐ The idea that I can never do anything right.
- ☐ Rejection, because no one could like me.
- ☐ Other: *the idea that I am not good enough*

I FIND IT HARD TO CONTROL THESE SEXUAL DESIRES:

- ☐ Pornography
- ☐ Sexual Fantasy.
- ☐ Masturbation.
- ☐ Homosexuality.
- ☐ Fornication/Adultery.
- ☐ Other: _____

I STRUGGLE WITH FEARS IN MY LIFE:

- ☐ Fear of sickness.
- ☐ Fear of death.
- ☐ Fear of committing suicide.
- ☐ Fear of insanity.
- ☐ Fear of being hurt emotionally.
- ☐ Other: _____

MATERIALISM IS A PROBLEM FOR ME:

- ☐ It is hard for me to resist buying things.
- ☐ I have serious credit card debt.
- ☐ I find it hard to be a generous giver.
- ☐ I love to accumulate wealth.
- ☐ Other: _____

SELF-DISCIPLINE IS A PROBLEM IN MY LIFE, I FIND IT:

- ☐ Hard to control my laziness.
- ☐ Hard to submit to others.
- ☐ Hard to be consistent in things that I need to do.
- ☐ Hard to control my tongue.
- ☐ Other: _____

ANSWERS FOR QUIZ ON PAGE FIVE:
1, Bethesda; 2, Pentecost; 3, Shem, Ham, Japheth; 4, Elijah; 5, Gideon; 6, Peter;
7, Second coming of Jesus; 8, Satan; 9, Word of God; 10, James; 11, Lot; 12, Capernaum; 13, John;
14, Aaron; 15, Lazarus; 16, Paul.

ANSWERS FOR QUIZ ON PAGE SIX:
1, Demas; 2, Job; 3, David; 4, Darius; 5, Tarsus; 6, Barnabus; 7, Book of Nehemiah; 8, Satan;
9, Holy of Holies; 10, Bethany; 11, Meshach; 12, Deborah; 13, Joseph; 14, Bethel;
15, Abigail; 16, Bartholomew.

Iron Sharpens Iron

God has made us relational beings. We need one another in order to become who we are meant to be. We cannot fully realize our humanity until we live in community. The entrance of sin destroys community. Cain envied his brother and eventually murdered him. After this, God asked Cain, *"Where is your brother Abel?" "I don't know,"* he replied. *"Am I my brother's keeper?"* (Genesis 4:9)

This is just the opposite of the attitude of those living in the Kingdom of God. *Living the Christian life means becoming responsible for someone you might otherwise ignore.* Yes! I am my brother's keeper! We need to be responsible for one another. *There must be mutual accountability and responsibility.*

Each person needs someone to be accountable to in order to be built up in the Christian life. For every Protégé, there must be a Mentor. The two need to meet regularly and be accountable to each other for their growth. It does not matter when you meet, how long you meet, or where you meet. The key is that you keep one another accountable for how you live your life as a Christian, a citizen of your country, and a member of your family. Because accountability is vital, you need to meet regularly in order for it to be effective. You must be constantly accountable to one another.

HAVE ANY OF THESE THINGS EVER HAPPENED TO YOU?
- You attended a meeting and were touched by the Holy Spirit. You responded by making a promise to God — then you forgot your promise as you went about your life.
- You made a resolution at the beginning of the year, but before the end of a few months, you forgot what your goals were.
- You made a promise to someone — maybe a member of your family — but didn't keep it. You may even have rationalized breaking your promise so that you would feel better about it.

We all need brothers and sisters to help us keep our promises. In order to keep one another accountable, we need to be honest with each other; we need to be transparent. Accountability is never a one-way affair. You cannot expect me to open my life to you and let you keep me in line if you never open your life to me. You and your Mentor will help each other keep promises.

At this stage, it is important for you to begin mentoring someone else. All you need is to be a few steps ahead. If you are not already a Mentor, make it your goal to become one as soon as possible.

☐ I am mentoring another Christian.
☐ I have yet to find a Protégé.

Your Journey Map

Congratulations! You are on the way. Remember, you need to keep on growing for the rest of your life. The Christian life is very exciting — it is never boring. Your whole life will be an adventure. Enjoy it. It gets better all the time. "All things work out for good!" Trust God and move ahead by faith.

The following section is your Journey Map. It shows you the next stages of your journey. It is good to know where you are going. After all, if you do not know where you're going, then how can you know when you get there? On the other hand, you can be certain that God has other items He will add to your training.

In high school, they have a series of required courses that everyone must go through. What Christians need to discover is that God has different courses for us to take alongside of life's requirements. He puts us together with certain students to teach us patience; He also puts us in situations where we must learn to care for others. You too have a Journey Map plotted out for you; be assured that there will be surprises on the way.

The following stages are crucial for every member of the church. Everyone needs the items mentioned below; they are foundational for every believer. Before you look at stops you must pass through for your journey on this stage, spend some time in prayer.

Dear Lord, I submit my life to you. I am saved by the blood of the lamb. I do not belong to myself — I belong to you. Help me to be more Christ-like as I continue on my journey of life. I want to grow in my life and glorify Your name. Amen.

On a scale of 1-5 mark how much each statement applies to your life:
[1] meaning that this doesn't apply to your life at all, and [5] meaning that you have fully done what the statement says.

_____ **A NEW SET OF VALUES**
I am not only a citizen of a new Kingdom with a new set of values, but also positively rebuilding each of my major values according to those of this new Kingdom.

_____ **GENEROUS GIVING**
I am a steward of the money that God has entrusted to my care, and I give generously and regularly.

DEPENDENCE ON GOD THROUGH CONSISTENT PRAYER

____ I know how to pray and am demonstrating my dependence on God by consistently talking to Him in prayer. I am responding to the circumstances in life by praying.

LISTENING TO THE VOICE OF GOD

____ I listen to the voice of God, and I seek Him in all life's situations. I obey the leading of God in my life.

ACTIVELY PARTICIPATING IN YOUR CHURCH

____ I am actively seeking to build up and preserve the unity of my church, and I am actively participating in a cell group.

A SPIRIT-DIRECTED LIFE

____ I realize that it is essential to be filled with the Holy Spirit and am consistently experiencing this filling. I am living a Spirit-directed life.

FEEDING ON THE WORD OF GOD

____ I am regularly feeding on the Word of God. I consistently memorize the Scriptures and have a basic understanding of the Bible.

WORSHIPPING GOD

____ I am experiencing the presence of God and finding joy in both private and corporate worship.

RESPONDING WITH THANKSGIVING

____ I am thankful for all things because I have a positive perspective on life and ministry that is based on the promises of God.

BUILDING STRONG AND HARMONIOUS RELATIONSHIPS

____ I have strong relationships with others — living in harmony with those in my cell group and family. I am open to others, especially to my cell members and Mentor.

DEMONSTRATING CHRIST

____ I demonstrate Christ at my place of work (or school) with integrity.

_____ **A WILLINGNESS TO SERVE OTHERS**
I know the importance of imitating Christ and am demonstrating a willingness to serve others even in menial tasks.

_____ **MINISTERING TO OTHERS BY USING THE GIFTS OF THE SPIRIT**
I am using the gifts to build up fellow believers and am participating in the ministry times both in the cell group and the celebrations.

_____ **CONFRONTING SATANIC INFLUENCES IN OTHERS**
I have learned to confront the power of Satan in the lives of others and am prevailing against these forces, especially in the lives of fellow cell members.

_____ **SENSITIVE TO THE NEEDS OF OTHERS**
I am sensitive of the needs of the people around me, especially those in my cell group, and am taking the initiative to care and pray for them.

_____ **PRAYING AND REACHING OUT TO THE LOST**
I have a heart to win the lost for Christ and am praying for my unbelieving friends and family members on a regular basis.

_____ **ACTIVELY WITNESSING TO OTHERS ABOUT CHRIST**
I actively testify to the goodness of God in my life and in the lives of other Christians. I share the Gospel when there is opportunity.

_____ **FOLLOWING-UP ON NEW BELIEVERS**
I know how to follow-up a new believer and mentor a new Christian.

_____ **DEVELOPING A HEART FOR MISSIONS**
I am concerned for unreached people in other parts of the world. I have either supported a cell member to go on a mission trip or have attended one myself.

_____ **SETTING GOALS**
I know how to develop yearly growth goals for myself.

Your Journey Map

The following are the items of your Spiritual Journey as a Growing Christian. Check [✓] three items that you feel you need to have in your life in the immediate future. Your evaluation in the last three pages and your present life situation can help you make the decision.

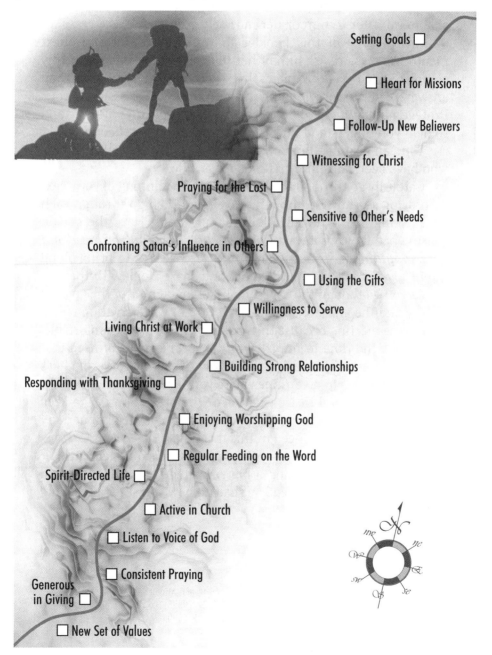

Setting Goals ☐

☐ Heart for Missions

☐ Follow-Up New Believers

☐ Witnessing for Christ

Praying for the Lost ☐

☐ Sensitive to Other's Needs

Confronting Satan's Influence in Others ☐

☐ Using the Gifts

☐ Willingness to Serve

Living Christ at Work ☐

☐ Building Strong Relationships

Responding with Thanksgiving ☐

☐ Enjoying Worshipping God

☐ Regular Feeding on the Word

Spirit-Directed Life ☐

☐ Active in Church

☐ Listen to Voice of God

☐ Consistent Praying

Generous in Giving ☐

☐ New Set of Values

Instructions for the Mentor

The Journey Guide for Growing Christians is designed to help you understand the spiritual, emotional, and intellectual background of your Protégé. Once you learn these things you will be able to minister to him or her more effectively.

Give a copy of this booklet to your Protégé at your next mentoring session. Ask him or her to take it home and prayerfully complete each page. Explain that there are no right or wrong answers. The purpose of going through the booklet is to help your Protégé pinpoint where he or she is on the spiritual journey and to help you understand how to mentor him or her effectively.

You can also use this *Journey Guide* with new cell members who have been faithful Christians for awhile.

Carefully go through the booklet at the beginning of your next mentoring session. Begin with prayer, and then go through each page asking if your Protégé has any questions. Have the person share what they wrote and why. *Assure him that he need not share anything he is not ready to share.* Feel free to bring along a *Journey Guide* that you filled out and share along with them.

As you go though the pages, make a mental note of the areas of victory and the areas of special need. Do not write anything down during the meeting because this makes people very uncomfortable. This is not the time to minister to the specific areas of need that arise as you move through the booklet. That will come in God's time. The point is to determine where your Protégé is on his or her spiritual journey and to see what he or she needs in order to keep progressing. You might pray for one or two specific needs, but don't expect to address every need in this meeting.

End your time together with prayer and encouragement. For some people they are taking a big risk in sharing their life with you. Encourage your Protégé by sharing how you see God moving in his of her life.

Copyright © 2001 by TOUCH® Outreach Ministries
P. O. Box 19888, Houston, TX 77224-9888, U.S.A.
(281) 497-7901 • Fax (281) 497-0904
Find us on the World Wide Web at *http://www.touchusa.org*